A Promise Made

Written by Jonathan Lau

Illustrated by Mike Lee

The golden sun is on the rise.
The faithful clock loudly cries.

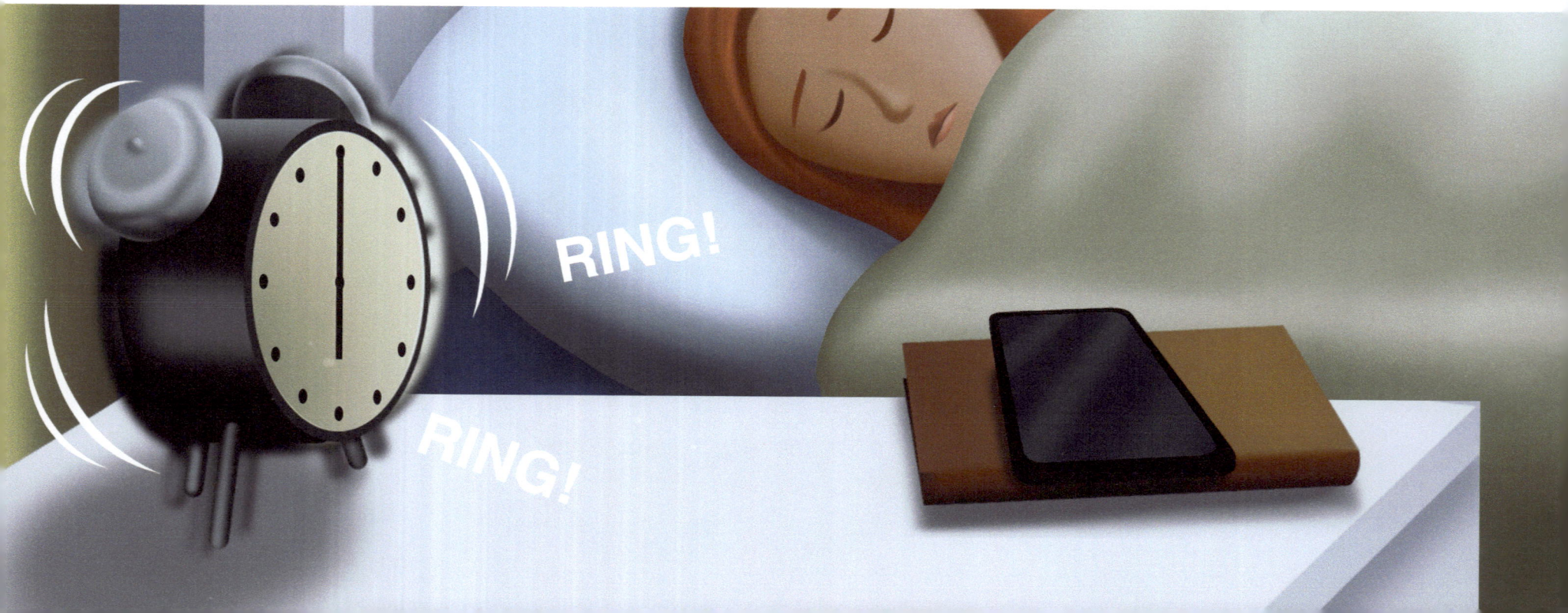

RING!

RING!

With a smile, son waves, bright-eyed and bushy tailed.
With a stretch, Mom yawns, and then a long exhale.

ring! —

ring! —

"Dad, tomorrow's my birthday! Will you be back?"

"There's snow on the ground, much more than a flurry, but I promise to be home, so no need to worry!"

"Good news, Son. Yes, my plane's on the tarmac!"

"Attention all passengers: flights are canceled today!"

"This is awful news! What will my son say?"

But a promise was made, and promises are kept;
Dad will find a new way, and so away he steps.

EXIT

CHOO!

CHOO!

TAXI

A heavy train is picking up the pace,
And running is hard with a large suitcase.

"Look who we have here..."

"A new member of our band!"

They quickly put a cowbell in his hand.

With a jolt, the train comes to a sudden stop.
Huge rocks are falling from a nearby hilltop.

Dad's fear of heights does not stop him one bit.
He carefully climbs to the top of it.

From up high he looks; home is finally in sight,
But getting there will take every ounce of Dad's might.

Quietly he creeps, he cannot make a sound.
The bears are all snoozing, so he tiptoes around.

Then out of the forest, Dad sees a big road,
And along comes a truck with an unpleasant load.

Without a second thought, Dad hops up inside.
For walking is worse than this pig-loaded ride.

"This is our stop," says the driver to Dad. It's a family of farmers who seem to love plaid.

The farmer's girl has a bike to sell. "I'll take it," Dad says, "with a basket and bell!"

Wobbly and slow, and bit by bit,
Tired legs will not make Dad quit!

With tires now flat, it is time to walk,
But Dad is close, he is on the right block.

There's a cute little dog, all fluffy and black.

bark!

bark!

But before Dad knows it, he is under attack!

Finally he's home, but the front door is locked!

And it's far too late to give a big knock.

Dad sits down to give his tired feet a break.

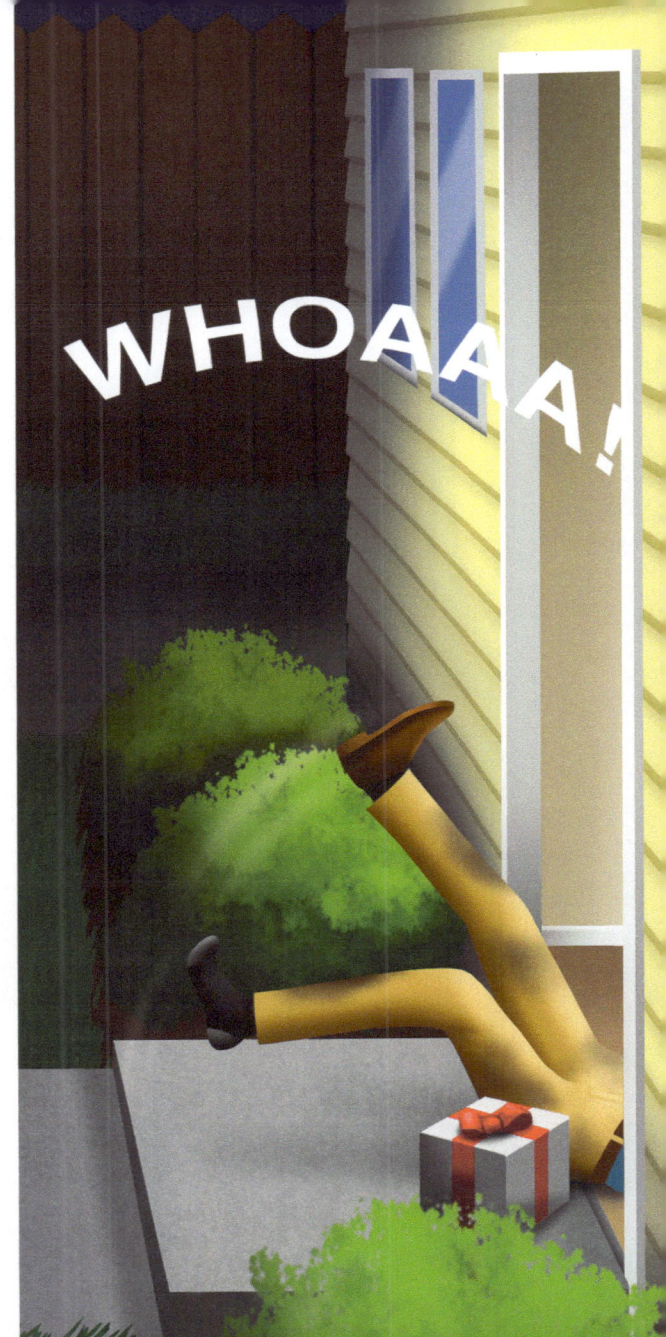

WHOAAA!

When there stands his son, who is still wide awake.

Dad is tired and messy, and a little delayed,
But his son always knew he'd keep the promise he made.

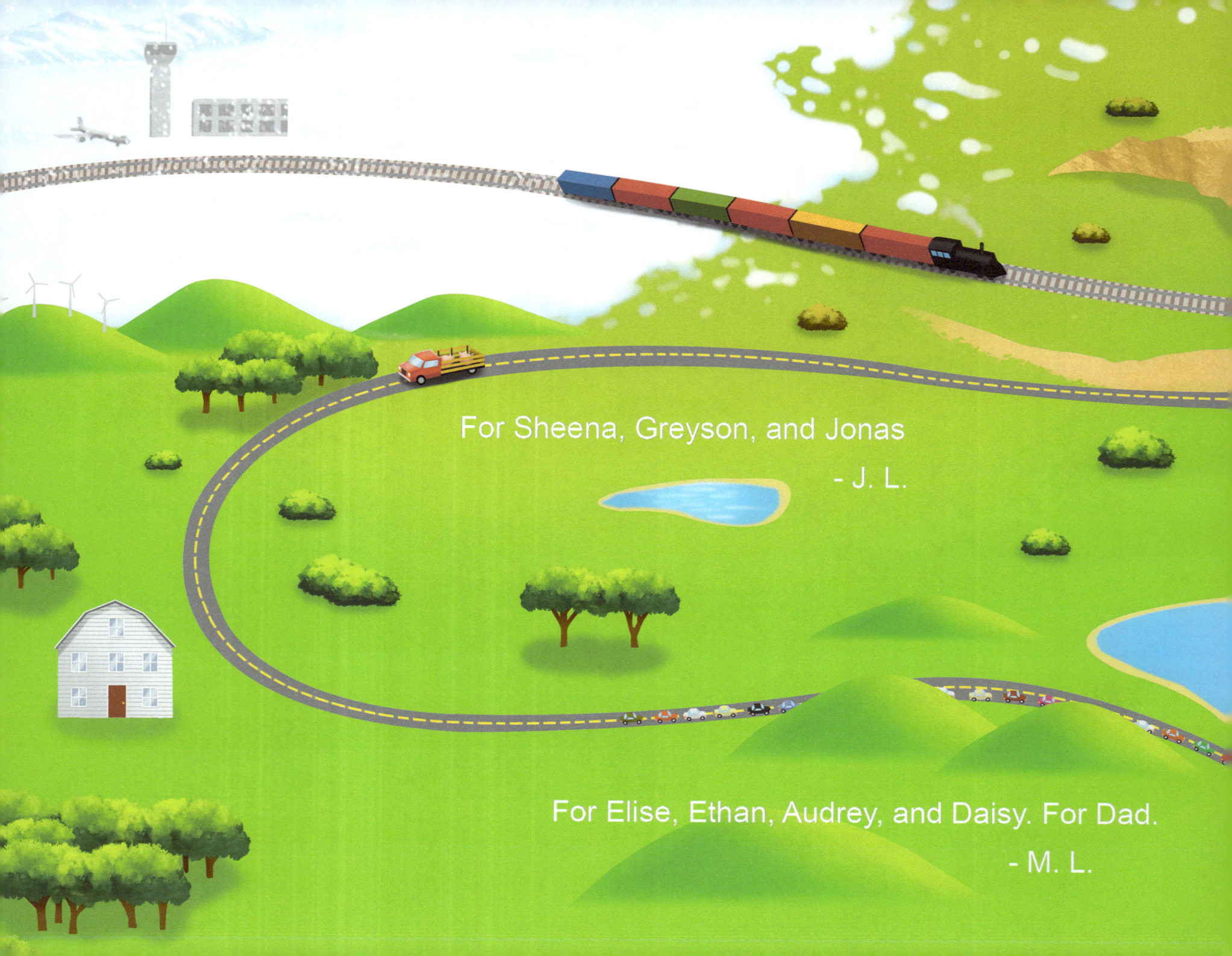

For Sheena, Greyson, and Jonas

- J. L.

For Elise, Ethan, Audrey, and Daisy. For Dad.

- M. L.

Library of Congress Cataloging-in-Publication Data in process at the time of publication (2019)

Library of Congress Control Number: 2019940327

ISBN: 9781734168808

Printed in the United States of America

Questions to consider asking your children:

What do you think is a promise?

What did the dad promise his son?

How do you think the son felt when his dad kept his promise by coming home?

Why is it important for everyone to try and keep promises they've made?

Easter Eggs:

Can you find these animals and objects?

x4   x3

www.ingramcontent.com/pod-product-compliance
Lightning Source LLC
Chambersburg PA
CBHW040406100426

42811CB00017B/1853